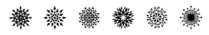

The Marriage Advice Journal

Words of wisdom from friends, family and
your own experiences on how to make the
most of your marriage.

Also by LoveBook™:

The Original "LoveBook™"
Create a custom gift book listing all of the reasons you love someone...we print it, bind it & ship it.

The Activity Book for Couples
Whether you are just dating or have been together for 50 years, these fun games and drawing activities are sure to bring laughter to your day!

The Romantic Coupon Book
A fun, romantic coupon book for anyone in love. This humorous coupon book will give your lover discounts and freebies that will keep you occupied for months! Contains 22 beautifully illustrated coupons.

The Bucket List for Couples
An exciting book to help couples come up with a list of goals that you'd like to achieve together. It includes categories, goal ideas, and pages to document your completed goals. A great way to spend time with your significant other while accomplishing amazing things.

All of these titles and more can be found at
www.LoveBookOnline.com

The Marriage Advice Journal

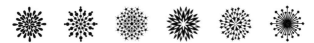

Words of wisdom from friends, family and
your own experiences on how to make the
most of your marriage.

Published by Neuron Publishing
www.neuronpublishing.com
www.LoveBookOnline.com

For

....

With Love From

....

Date

....

Why Use This Journal?

The purpose of this journal is to gather advice, anecdotes and wisdom about love and marriage from those who have been in all types of relationships, are any age, and have differing viewpoints. Hopefully their knowledge will help you in your journey towards a loving and lasting relationship.

Each section is clearly labeled with different aspects of relationships, and can include all of the following subtopics, or more that may not be listed here:

* Feeding the Marriage: growing together, cooking, putting effort into the relationship

* Keeping the Spark: intimacy, sex, trying new things, learning about each other

* Working Through Problems: family issues, solving problems, working together

* Adding to the Family: raising children, having pets, expanding the home, dealing with family

* General Words of Wisdom: covers any of the above topics and more

The last section titled "My Experiences" is meant for you, the owner of this journal, to document your own experiences throughout your marriage. In the future, share these with your children, grandchildren or others who are getting married and help spread the love!

Contents

Feeding the Marriage

"Love is like a tree, it grows of its own accord, it puts down deep roots into our whole being."

~ *Victor Hugo*

Feeding the Marriage

Feeding the Marriage

Feeding the Marriage

Feeding the Marriage

Feeding the Marriage

_____
_____
_____
_____
_____
_____
_____
_____
_____
_____
_____
_____
_____
_____
_____
_____
_____
_____
_____
_____
_____
_____
_____
_____
_____
_____
_____

Feeding the Marriage

Feeding the Marriage

Feeding the Marriage

Feeding the Marriage

_____

Feeding the Marriage

Feeding the Marriage

Keeping the Spark

"No matter how much cats
fight, there always seems to
be plenty of kittens."

~ Abraham Lincoln

Keeping the Spark

Keeping the Spark

Keeping the Spark

Keeping the Spark

Keeping the Spark

Keeping the Spark

Keeping the Spark

Keeping the Spark

Keeping the Spark

Keeping the Spark

Keeping the Spark

Working Through Problems

"Love is not love that alters
when it alteration finds."

~ William Shakespeare

Working Through Problems

Working Through Problems

Working Through Problems

Working Through Problems

Working Through Problems

Working Through Problems

Working Through Problems

Working Through Problems

Working Through Problems

Working Through Problems

Working Through Problems

Adding to the Family

"We never know the love of a parent
till we become parents ourselves."

~ *Henry Ward Beecher*

Adding to the Family

Adding to the Family

Adding to the Family

Adding to the Family

Adding to the Family

Adding to the Family

Adding to the Family

Adding to the Family

Adding to the Family

Adding to the Family

Adding to the Family

General Words of Wisdom

"Soulmates are people who bring out
the best in you. They are not perfect,
but are always perfect for you."

~ *Author Unknown*

General Words of Wisdom

General Words of Wisdom

General Words of Wisdom

General Words of Wisdom

General Words of Wisdom

General Words of Wisdom

General Words of Wisdom

General Words of Wisdom

General Words of Wisdom

76

General Words of Wisdom

General Words of Wisdom

General Words of Wisdom

My Own Experiences

"Let your love be like the
misty rains, coming softly,
but flooding the river."

~ *Malagasy Proverb*

My Own Experiences

My Own Experiences

My Own Experiences

My Own Experiences

My Own Experiences

My Own Experiences

My Own Experiences

My Own Experiences

My Own Experiences

My Own Experiences

My Own Experiences

My Own Experiences

My Own Experiences

My Own Experiences

My Own Experiences

About LoveBook™

We are a group of individuals who want to spread love in all its forms. We believe love fuels the world and every relationship is important. We hope this books helps build on that belief.

CPSIA information can be obtained at www.ICGtesting.com
Printed in the USA
BVOW032355080812

297431BV00002B/1/P